W9-AHX-814

Author:
Jacqueline Morley studied English literature at Oxford University. She has taught English and history and now works as a freelance writer. She has written historical fiction and nonfiction for children.

Artist:
Mark Bergin was born in Hastings, England, in 1961. He studied at Eastbourne College of Art and specializes in historical reconstructions, aviation, and maritime subjects. He lives in Bexhill-on-Sea, England, with his wife and children.

Series creator:
David Salariya was born in Dundee, Scotland. He has illustrated a wide range of books and has created and designed many new series for publishers in the UK and overseas. David established The Salariya Book Company in 1989. He lives in Brighton with his wife, illustrator Shirley Willis, and their son, Jonathan.

Editor: **Stephen Haynes**

Editorial Assistant: **Mark Williams**

Published in Great Britain in 2013 by
The Salariya Book Company Ltd
25 Marlborough Place, Brighton BN1 1UB

ISBN-13: 978-0-531-25942-9 (lib. bdg.)   978-0-531-23039-8 (pbk.)

All rights reserved.
Published in 2013 in the United States
by Franklin Watts
An imprint of Scholastic Inc.
Published simultaneously in Canada.

A CIP catalog record for this book is available
from the Library of Congress.

Printed and bound in Shanghai, China.
Printed on paper from sustainable sources.
Reprinted in 2014.
3 4 5 6 7 8 9 10 R 22 21 20 19 18 17 16 15 14

PAPER FROM SUSTAINABLE FORESTS

You Wouldn't Want to Explore with Lewis and Clark!

Written by
Jacqueline Morley

Illustrated by
Mark Bergin

Created and designed by
David Salariya

An Epic Journey You'd Rather Not Make

Franklin Watts®
An Imprint of Scholastic Inc.
NEW YORK • TORONTO • LONDON • AUCKLAND • SYDNEY
MEXICO CITY • NEW DELHI • HONG KONG
DANBURY, CONNECTICUT

Contents

Introduction

It's 1803, and Thomas Jefferson, the third president of the United States, has commissioned an expedition to find a route across North America from the Atlantic to the Pacific, through the territory known as the Louisiana Purchase. If a way through the wilderness can be found, American traders can capture the rich Pacific coast fur trade and establish U.S. rights to the land. Then the American nation can expand across the whole continent. This is President Jefferson's dream.

Most members of the expedition are soldiers in the U.S. Army, and you are one of them. What hardships await you on your epic journey?

Nobody's made this journey before. Who knows what we'll find?

IN 1783, the British colonies in North America became officially independent with the signing of the Treaty of Paris. This new country, the United States, was about a quarter of its present size, covering much of the eastern part of the continent as far as the Mississippi River. The rest of the continent, including a vast unexplored wilderness to the west, was claimed by European nations.

The Way to the West

Jefferson has appointed a young army officer, Captain Meriwether Lewis, to lead the expedition. Lewis's first task is to follow the Missouri River and discover its source in the Rocky Mountains. Few Europeans have seen the Rockies, but Native Americans have lived there for centuries. Beyond the mountains is the Columbia River. Lewis must find its source and travel down it to the Pacific Ocean.

On the journey he will meet many Native American peoples. He must try to persuade them to stop fighting one another and to trade with the Americans, rather than with the British.

William Clark

LEWIS HAS CHOSEN his old army colleague William Clark as the co-leader of the expedition.

LOUISIANA PURCHASE. In 1803, Napoleon Bonaparte, First Consul of France, agrees to sell the territory known as Louisiana to the United States. It is a vast tract of land, many times larger than the present-day state of Louisiana.

PRESIDENT JEFFERSON is an expert on science and technology. He shows Lewis how to take astronomical measurements to help plot the course of the expedition.

AMERICAN SHIPS have been trading furs on the north Pacific coast for a number of years. In 1792, a trader found the mouth of the Columbia River.

If we sell it to the Americans, at least the British won't get it.

Mouth of Columbia River

CANADA (British)

Rocky Mountains

Missouri

LOUISIANA

SPANISH TERRITORY

Mississippi

Ohio

Main areas of European settlement

Handy Hint

Learn all you can about botany and zoology. There are exciting new discoveries to be made.

This French map is not very clear, Mr. President.

Once you've been there, we can make better maps.

Lewis and Jefferson discuss their plans at the president's home, Monticello, near Charlottesville, Virginia.

I made the cut!

VOLUNTEERS are chosen and sworn in as soldiers for the trip. They have to be tough!

Stocking Up

Lewis sails down the Ohio River to meet Clark. The two captains, with a crew of about 15, then set off in two small pirogues (open boats) and a larger keelboat (river barge). They reach the Mississippi in November 1803. But they are running late because the keelboat was finished later than planned. They can't continue up the Missouri River, because it freezes in winter.

So the team has to spend the winter camped near St. Louis. Here they train for life in the wilderness. The keelboat is awkward to handle, so the captains take on more crew members. That means buying more supplies and weapons, too.

IN MAY 1804, the boats are loaded with goods. It's important to take items that can be traded with the Native Americans: glass beads, mirrors, blankets, needles, scissors, knives, and trinkets.

THE HEAVY KEELBOAT proves hard to steer in the changing currents of the river. It often gets stuck on sandbars and other obstacles and has to be hauled clear.

MOSQUITOES are everywhere! They get into the men's eyes, noses, ears, and throats. You can keep them away only with smoke from the campfire or by smearing yourself with grease.

By the time they set off up the Missouri on May 14, 1804, the two captains have a team of approximately 45 men, including an interpreter and Clark's black slave, York.

Across the Plains

The expedition inches its way upriver, between lush prairies. It travels around 20 miles (32 kilometers) on a good day, but much less when strong currents prevent rowing and the team has to struggle with towlines along the riverbanks.

By August you are entering a vast grassland (present-day South Dakota), home to many Plains Indian cultures. Here the captains get their first chance to deliver the president's peace message. It gets a mixed welcome, especially from the Sioux, who resent white traders.

HUNTING PARTIES go out regularly to get food. The crew first tastes bison on August 23. Hardworking crew members eat 9 pounds (4 kg) of meat a day!

THE PLAINS teem with wildlife, such as beaver in the streams, elk and deer in the woods by the river, and herds of bison out on the open plains.

THE OTOE listen politely to Lewis, but they seem baffled. Why should they stop fighting? How else can warriors win glory? But they accept gifts and are presented with medals showing President Jefferson's head.

Bison (also called American buffalo)

Pronghorn

Jackrabbit

Coyote

Beaver

Prairie dogs

Guilty!

COURT MARTIAL. By August the strains of the trip are beginning to show. Private Reed tries to desert. After three days he is caught, tried, and sentenced to a whipping.

Handy Hint

Have fun when you can. Lewis's birthday, the same day as the court martial, is a good excuse for a party.

We don't want your kind here.

THE SIOUX try to stop you from coming onto their territory, but back down when they see that you have guns.

A Harsh Winter

By late October 1804, with winter closing in, you are in an area that will later be called North Dakota. Your aim is to reach winter quarters at a group of villages belonging to the Hidatsa and Mandan peoples. This is the farthest point along the Missouri that white traders have visited.

When you get there, you are snowed in for five months. Fortunately, the Mandan and their chief Sheheke are welcoming and you get along well with them. On New Year's Day some of the crew dance for the Mandan. York is considered the best dancer.

SACAGAWEA (pronounced sa-KAH-ga-WEE-a), a young Shoshone woman, joins the team as an interpreter. She is 16, and about to have a baby. Her husband, French-Canadian trader Toussaint Charbonneau, also comes.

THE MANDAN are farmers, not nomads. Mandan women paddle circular "bull boats" made of bison hide stretched over a wooden frame.

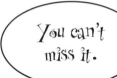

You can't miss it.

THE HIDATSA describe the way ahead. You will come to a huge waterfall, and then to the mountains where the Shoshone people live.

THE WINTER of 1804 to 1805 is bitterly cold. The frozen Missouri River becomes a highway for the Mandan sleds, and for huge herds of bison.

York

Handy Hint

Ask the Mandan to show you how they hunt on horseback. They ride at breakneck speed!

FOOD SUPPLIES are getting low, and you are running out of goods to trade. So the expedition's blacksmith makes axes for the Mandan in exchange for corn.

ON APRIL 7, 1805, the keelboat is sent back east. The rest of the team—now including Sacagawea's baby son—sets off into unknown territory.

13

The Great Falls

The team—now 30 men, plus a mother and baby—sets off in the two pirogues and six dugout canoes. Here the plains are home to wolves and grizzly bears. The river runs under cliffs that come right to the water's edge. Headwinds batter the boats. As you help to tow them through rocky shallows, your back is burned by the sun, your legs numbed by the icy water. On June 13, 1805, you reach the Great Falls of the Missouri—not the one waterfall that the Hidatsa described, but a series of five, stretching for more than 12 miles (20 km). The boats have to be transported overland in blistering heat.

Majestically grand scenery!*

Lewis's own words, from his journal

ON MAY 14, one of the boats nearly capsizes. Sacagawea calmly rescues the things that have fallen overboard, including precious notes and sketches.

ON MAY 26, Lewis climbs to the top of the cliffs and sees distant snowcapped peaks glistening in the sun—his first sight of the fabled Rocky Mountains!

Arooooo

GRAY WOLVES are a common sight here. Packs of them lie in wait for a stray bison calf or a sick bison that can't keep up with the herd.

Handy Hint

Always have a weapon handy. Lewis scared away a bear by jumping into the river and waving a spear.

THE RIVER carries you past tall cliffs worn away by wind and rain into all kinds of odd shapes. Bighorn sheep perch on the rocky peaks.

SPECIAL CARRIAGES have to be made to haul the boats around the falls. The whole operation takes a month. When it is windy, the boats' sails can be used to help speed travel.

SACAGAWEA falls seriously ill, and Clark nurses her back to health. Then, when a flash flood sweeps down a gully, she is nearly drowned.

Into the Rockies

By August 1805, you are high in the Rockies, where the river has shrunk to a stream. Boulders and rapids make canoe travel impossible. The plan is to cross the summit on horseback and make new canoes on the other side. But first you have to find horses! The Hidatsa have told you that the local Shoshone have horses for sale—but there are no Shoshone anywhere. If you can't get across the Rockies before it snows, you'll be in serious trouble.

THE CANOES enter the Rockies through a deep canyon (above).

A SMOKE SIGNAL (below) shows that the local people are close by, but don't want to meet you.

THE TEAM is near the breaking point from heat, sickness, and the effort of dragging the canoes in the strong current. You can't manage to travel more than 4 miles (6 km) a day.

We only want to buy some horses!

ON AUGUST 11, a Shoshone rider is seen in the distance, but he gallops off when Lewis approaches.

NEARING the summit of the Rockies, the mighty Missouri River is reduced to a trickle. Private McNeal boasts that he can stand astride it.

Handy Hint

Don't step on a prickly pear cactus, as Clark did. His thin moccasins did not protect him.

Aaaargh!

Sacagawea tells the story of how she was captured by Hidatsa raiders and sold to her husband, Charbonneau. She speaks in Hidatsa, and Charbonneau translates.

She says they took her friends, too.

Meeting the Shoshone

Beyond the summit Lewis finally meets the Shoshone. They are welcoming, but wary of selling him horses. They fear he may be allied with their enemies, the Blackfeet.

But the Shoshone chief, Cameahwait (pronounced CAME-a-WAIT), agrees to come and meet the other members of the expedition, if only to prove that he's not a coward. His trust is rewarded: among the strangers he finds his long-lost sister, Sacagawea!

CAMEAHWAIT embraces Lewis as a sign of friendship.

HE WARNS LEWIS that there are rapids ahead and the boats will not be able to pass.

ON SEPTEMBER 1, the expedition sets off along a mountain trail used by the Nez Perce, a Native American people who live farther west. An elderly Shoshone goes with the group as a guide. The Shoshone have agreed to sell the expedition horses, but the price is steep.

FASCINATED by the expedition members with their boats and guns, the Shoshone agree to help them. Using Shoshone horses and homemade saddles, the team crosses the pass while the Shoshone carry most of the gear.

I know all the trails.

18

A Real Crisis

Y ou thought the Rockies were just one range of mountains, but now you discover that they are a whole series of tightly packed ranges. Your guide (you call him Old Toby) leads you along narrow ridges and down steep slopes. Horses and men struggle constantly to keep their footing. In some places there is no trail, and even Toby gets slightly lost. He tells you that if you had taken a different route from the Great Falls in the first place you could have completed the journey in five days instead of 51!

Your supplies are almost exhausted when at last you find a Nez Perce village. Its people lead you to the westward-flowing Clearwater River.

IN THE BITTERROOT RANGE you find hot springs where water that is almost boiling spouts from the rocks.

FOOD STOCKS are so low that you have to kill one of the horses for food.

I hate to have to do this.

It's him or us.

THE HORSE carrying Clark's desk loses its footing and falls 130 feet (40 meters). The horse survives but the desk doesn't.

THE EXHAUSTED TEAM discusses whether to give up or go on. But it has no choice. Everyone is too weak now to go back the way they came.

I hope he's as good as he says he is.

Handy Hint
You'll have to leave the horses behind. Brand them so you know which ones are yours.

It's this way, I'm sure.

CHIEF TWISTED HAIR of the Nez Perce helps Clark find tall trees and make them into canoes. The tree trunks are hollowed out with a slow-burning fire.

21

The Columbia River

Overjoyed to be on the river again, the captains are now eager to keep moving at all costs. The Clearwater is a swift-flowing mountain river, full of rapids that you shoot recklessly. The canoes are then swept into the powerful Snake River, which flows west through deep canyons. On October 18, you finally enter the Columbia River. The local Chinook people look on in amazement as you shoot the fearsome rapids. At last the end of your journey is in sight! Your triumphant team of explorers is approaching the Pacific coast.

The Dalles is a terrifying series of falls and rapids on the Columbia River. When the going becomes too dangerous, you have to get out of the canoes and lower them through the falls by rope.

There's barely room to swing a paddle!

Handy Hint

If you can hear the sound of waves breaking on rocks, you must be near the sea.

THE NEZ PERCE are expert at catching salmon. You live on dried salmon until you are sick of it.

PASSING BEACON ROCK on November 3, 1805, you realize the sea is near, because the river is beginning to rise and fall with the tide.

THE CAPTAINS visit the lodge of a Chinook chief.

YOU MEET NATIVE AMERICANS in European clothes. They have been trading with the British.

CLARK IS IMPRESSED by the Chinook's carved and painted canoes. He sketches them in his journal.

On the Pacific Coast

After weeks camped on the Columbia estuary, the team finds a sheltered spot for a winter home. You name it Fort Clatsop after the local Native American people. The Clatsop are welcoming and willing to sell food, but you have very few goods left to trade with them.

You had hoped to find an American ship that could take you home, or a trading post where you could buy goods on credit. But there is no sign of either. You will have to go back the way you came!

LEWIS EXPLORES the north shore of the estuary. At the point where it meets the sea, he carves his name on a tree.

THE CLATSOP offer to sell a beautiful robe of sea otter fur. The price: Sacagawea's belt of blue beads.

Who wants to try the other bank?

THE TEAM VOTES on whether to move camp. Everyone has a vote, including York and Sacagawea.

THE CLATSOP visit regularly to sell food, but they are not trusted to stay in the fort at night.

24

The journals are your most precious cargo. Scientists back east are eager to learn about your discoveries.

AT FORT CLATSOP Clark writes in his journals. He includes sketches of wildlife and of the special cradle used by the Chinook to flatten their babies' foreheads. A flattened head is a sign of high status for the Chinook.

In January 1806, a whale is washed up on shore. By the time Clark and his team arrive, the Clatsop have already stripped off the blubber.

A Hero's Welcome

By May 1806, you have collected the horses that you left with the Nez Perce and you have headed back into the mountains. The trail is blocked by snow, but you are rescued and guided by some Nez Perce. The party then splits up. You go with Lewis to explore a muddy river that you saw last year. There you have the expedition's only serious clash with Native Americans. Clark heads down the Yellowstone River to the Missouri, where the two teams meet up again. Two months later you all return to St. Louis to a hero's welcome.

MEANWHILE, Sacagawea is guiding Clark's party from the Three Forks to the Yellowstone River. This is her home country and she knows it well.

CLARK'S PARTY travels at top speed down the Yellowstone on a raft supported by two huge tree trunks. It is big enough to carry them all.

LEWIS and three of his men meet a party of eight Blackfeet warriors. They are not inviting, but eventually the two parties agree to camp together.

IN THE MORNING the Blackfeet try to steal your rifles and horses. In the scuffle, one of the Blackfeet is fatally stabbed and another is hit by a bullet.

Aaargh! I don't even look like an elk!

FRIENDLY FIRE. Lewis is accidentally shot in the backside by one of his men while hunting elk.

Handy Hint

Don't stay and fight the Blackfeet. It's safer to flee.

We made it!

On September 23, 1806, most of St. Louis turns out to meet the returning heroes.

What Happened Next?

With your help, Lewis and Clark have achieved almost everything that President Jefferson hoped for. They have mapped the way to the Pacific and made many new scientific discoveries. Unfortunately, the route is far more difficult than Jefferson had imagined. Instead of an easy waterway, you found "tremendous mountains which for 60 miles [100 km] are covered with eternal snows." But you also found rivers with more beavers "than any other streams on earth." This news sends fur trappers rushing westward to make their fortunes along the Missouri River.

FUR TRAPPERS flourish in the Louisiana Territory, living and hunting in the wilderness.

IN 1824, Jedediah Smith rediscovers an easier route through the Rockies that had been found in 1812 by Robert Stuart. South Pass becomes known as the Gateway to the West.

MERIWETHER LEWIS (1774–1809) is made governor of the Louisiana Territory. He dies suddenly at the age of 35. It is most likely a suicide.

WILLIAM CLARK (1770–1838) becomes superintendent of Indian Affairs for the Louisiana Territory. He eventually, but very reluctantly, grants freedom to his slave York.

SACAGAWEA and her husband, Toussaint Charbonneau, stay with the Mandan. A few years later, their son Jean-Baptiste goes east with Clark to be educated. He visits Europe before returning to America to become a trapper. In 2001, Sacagawea is posthumously made an honorary sergeant in the U.S. Army.

Handy Hint

Go west, young man! Thousands will travel to the West Coast in search of fortune.

Sheheke, the Mandan chief who welcomed Lewis and Clark, travels with them to Washington, D.C., in 1806 and is introduced to President Jefferson.

Glossary

Bison (commonly called American buffalo) A large wild ox. Enormous herds lived on the North American Plains until the mid-1800s, when white settlers shot almost all of them.

Blackfeet A Plains Indian people of the upper Missouri, greatly feared for their violent treatment of neighbors.

Blubber The fat of a whale.

Botany The scientific study of plants.

Brand To mark livestock with a red-hot piece of metal, as proof of ownership.

Bull boat A small circular boat made of wood and bison hide, used for fishing or river travel.

Canyon A steep-sided river valley.

Capsize (of a boat) To overturn.

Chinook A people of the lower Columbia River who lived by salmon fishing and hunting.

Clatsop A group in the Chinook nation.

Court martial A trial held by a military court.

Dalles, The A point on the Columbia River where huge rocks caused mighty rapids.

Estuary The mouth of a river, where tidal waters meet the river's current.

Flash flood A sudden flood, often caused by heavy rainfall pouring into a narrow channel.

Gully A steep-sided channel formed by running water.

Hidatsa Plains Indian allies of the Mandan.

Keelboat A long riverboat, similar to a barge, used on the Mississippi and Missouri rivers for shipping goods.

Mandan Plains Indians of the upper Missouri who lived in villages, hunted bison, and farmed.

Moccasin A soft-soled slipper made of leather, worn by many native peoples of North America.

Nez Perce A people of the plateau land west of the Rockies. Their name is French for "pierced nose," though they did not pierce their noses.

Nomads People who move from place to place in order to farm or hunt.

Otoe Plains Indians of the lower Missouri.

Pass A gap in a mountain range through which travelers can cross.

Pirogue An open boat, with or without a sail.

Plains Indians Native American peoples of the Great Plains (the vast grasslands of central North America).

Posthumously Happening after death.

Prairies Rich, lush grasslands that once covered huge areas of North America.

Rapids A stretch of a river that flows steeply downhill. The water may be very rough, especially if there are rocks breaking the surface.

Shoshone A large group of Native American peoples living west of the Rocky Mountains who traditionally were hunter-gatherers. When horse ownership spread (from the Spanish) among Native Americans, some Shoshone groups rode seasonally to the Great Plains to hunt buffalo.

Sioux The dominant Plains Indian people of the lower Missouri. They were great warriors and enemies of the Mandan and the Hidatsa.

Winter quarters A camp made by travelers to live in during the winter, when it is too difficult or dangerous to continue traveling.

Zoology The scientific study of animals.

Index